THE
LUFTWAFFE
IN CAMERA

By the same author:
Instruments of Darkness
Aircraft versus Submarine
The Last Year of the Luftwaffe
Luftwaffe Handbook
Battle of Britain: The Hardest Day, 18 August 1940
Battle of Britain Day, 15 September 1940
The Spitfire Story
Spitfire at War (three volumes)
Battle over the Reich
Blitz on Britain
Harrier at War
Panavia Tornado
Air Battle Central Europe
The History of US Electronic Warfare (two volumes)

Written in co-operation with Jeff Ethell:
Target Berlin
World War II Fighting Jets
One Day in a Long War
Air War South Atlantic

THE
LUFTWAFFE
IN CAMERA

1939–1942

ALFRED PRICE

SUTTON PUBLISHING

First published in the United Kingdom in 1997 by
Sutton Publishing Limited · Phoenix Mill · Thrupp · Stroud · Gloucestershire

ISBN 0-7509-1635-4

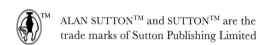

ALAN SUTTON™ and SUTTON™ are the
trade marks of Sutton Publishing Limited

Typeset in 11/15pt Baskerville.
Typesetting and origination by
Sutton Publishing Limited.
Printed in Great Britain by
Butler & Tanner, Frome, Somerset.

CONTENTS

INTRODUCTION

This book depicts, in photographs taken during the first three years of the Second World War, the Luftwaffe in its many aspects. The period September 1939 to September 1942 saw the force play a major part in securing a spectacular run of victories for German arms.

At the start of the war the Luftwaffe was one of the largest air forces in the world, and it was certainly the best equipped and trained. In each of the combat roles the aircraft types operated by the Luftwaffe were usually far superior to any enemy counterparts facing them. The sole exceptions were the Spitfire fighter and the Wellington bomber operated by the Royal Air Force. The performance of these planes was roughly equivalent to those of the Messerschmitt Bf 109 and the Heinkel He 111 respectively, although neither British type was yet available in large numbers.

In a series of carefully prepared Blitzkrieg offensives the German Army, with powerful air support, achieved breathtaking territorial gains over a twenty-month period. First Poland, then Denmark and Norway, then Holland, Belgium and France, and finally Yugoslavia and Greece were all defeated and occupied. The only serious setback for the Luftwaffe during this period was the Battle of Britain in the summer of 1940. Then, despite a long and hard-fought series of actions, the Luftwaffe failed to secure the air superiority over southern Britain that was an essential prerequisite for invasion. Yet, although the Luftwaffe incurred serious losses during the attacks on Britain, its reserves of aircraft and crews were sufficient to make good the gaps in its ranks. As a result the Luftwaffe emerged from the Battle of Britain as strong as it had been at the start of the campaign.

In June 1941 German forces launched yet another all-out Blitzkrieg offensive, this time against the Soviet Union. At first it seemed this would be merely a re-run of what had gone before. The German Army fought a series of large-scale enveloping actions, capturing millions of prisoners and vast quantities of military hardware. The Luftwaffe destroyed thousands of Soviet planes on the ground and in the air.

When it took part in a Blitzkrieg offensive, the Luftwaffe was expected to provide the maximum possible support for the army. By flying high daily sortie rates, and mounting low-altitude bombing and strafing attacks, it brought the full weight of its fire power to bear on enemy ground forces. Losses in aircraft and crews were accepted, and acceptable, provided the campaign could be brought to a rapid and victorious end.

At the start of the campaign in the East the Luftwaffe discovered a perplexing difference between this action and those fought earlier, however. In previous campaigns the enemy troops had 'gone to ground' when they came under air attack. The Soviet soldiers, in contrast, stood their ground and loosed off at their tormentors with any weapon that came to hand. In any one engagement there was only a very small chance that rifle or light machine-gun fire would bring down an aircraft. But, such was the pace of air operations, there were thousands of these encounters each week. As a result Luftwaffe losses began to mount.

At the end of the first hundred days of the offensive the Luftwaffe found itself in serious trouble. Over that period it had suffered an average daily loss of sixteen planes destroyed and ten damaged. Cumulatively, such a daily loss sustained over so long a period had disastrous consequences. The Luftwaffe lost just over 1,600 aircraft destroyed and a further 1,000 damaged, a total of 2,600 aircraft put out of action. That number was just short of the 2,770 combat planes it sent into action at the start of the campaign. In the same period the German aircraft industry produced about 2,200 combat planes. So the losses in aircraft destroyed

and damaged on the Eastern Front alone exceeded production by about 20 per cent. Of course, many damaged aircraft were repaired and put back into service. But that took time and the reserve of combat aircraft, assembled in aircraft parks before the campaign, was soon exhausted.

Only when the harsh Russian winter forced an end to large-scale air operations in that theatre, did the Luftwaffe get a respite. Then the depleted combat units could be withdrawn, in rotation, to rest and re-form. Losses fell sharply, allowing units to be restored to full strength with new and repaired aircraft. By February 1942 the immediate crisis had passed. However, it was a cruel portent of what could be expected when large-scale operations resumed on the Eastern Front later in the year. In December 1941 the USA entered the war on the side of the Allies. The US government moved rapidly to build up its forces and switch the nation's vast industrial capacity into armament production. Nevertheless, more than a year would elapse before US forces posed any significant direct threat to the Luftwaffe.

The hiatus in operations on the Eastern Front in the winter of 1941–42 allowed the Luftwaffe to strengthen its forces in other theatres. An influx of combat units into the Mediterranean area early in 1942 led to a rapid upsurge in activity there. Malta came under heavy air attack, and the highly effective blockade came close to starving the islanders into submission. In North Africa the revitalized Fliegerkorps Afrika supported the German Army in a succession of thrusts that took it almost to the gates of Cairo.

In the late spring of 1942 the ground dried out after the long Russian winter and spring thaw, allowing a resumption of large-scale operations. While the German Army made final preparations to resume its offensive, Luftwaffe units began concentrating in the theatre in readiness to provide support. After a long hard fight the German Army occupied the Crimea. In June the Panzers resumed their thrust eastward, heading for the valuable oilfields in the Caucasus area. Once again there were rapid initial advances, though not quite so rapid as those in the previous year. And yet again the Luftwaffe suffered heavy cumulative losses.

In September 1942 the territory occupied by German forces reached its greatest extent. The area under their control extended from Brittany in France to the Volga River in Russia, from the North Cape of Norway to the desert sands of Egypt.

Although the Luftwaffe was still an impressively strong fighting force, the first cracks in its edifice had begun to show. In terms of combat aircraft its numerical strength was a little larger than a year earlier, but the sum of its commitments was now far greater. The force was required to provide air support in three major but distant theatres of operations. In addition there was a large and growing home defence effort which tied down a quarter of its total fighter strength (including almost all its night fighters). In truth the Luftwaffe was now seriously overextended, with

scarcely any combat units in reserve to meet emergencies. The bulk of its forces were concentrated on the Eastern Front, but to achieve this it had had to cut to the bone the number of combat units in the West and in the Mediterranean area.

As serious as the severe numerical deficiencies in its strength, the Luftwaffe had to face the approaching obsolescence of many of its combat aircraft types. In September 1942 most of these were developed versions of designs that had entered service before the war. The Messerschmitt Bf 109 and Bf 110, the Junkers Ju 87 and Ju 88 and the Heinkel He 111, which equipped the lion's share of the combat units, were near the end of their development lives.

Two important new combat aircraft production programmes, which should have yielded sizable numbers of modern machines, had gone awry. The Messerschmitt Me 210 was to replace the Bf 110 in the long-range fighter, night fighter, fighter-bomber and reconnaissance roles, and also the Ju 87 as a dive-bomber. Yet the new plane's handling characteristics proved to be so bad that the programme had to be abandoned. The Heinkel He 177 four-engined heavy bomber had gone into service with one Gruppe, but its teething troubles were so severe that the type had to be withdrawn for extensive modifications. The only major new types to enter service since the beginning of the war were the Focke Wulf Fw 190 fighter and the Dornier Do 217 medium bomber; neither type was available in large numbers. In the absence of the replacement types planned for them, most Luftwaffe flying units had to soldier on with their ageing equipment. In stark contrast, each of the opposing air forces was introducing new combat planes that had long development lives ahead of them.

The problems facing the Luftwaffe did not end there. Since the start of the campaign in the East, the losses in aircrew had exceeded those being turned out by the training organization. The reserve of trained crews was exhausted and many units were now under-strength in flying personnel. Other pressures on the training organization exacerbated the difficulty. The Soviet offensive, early in 1942, left German troops surrounded at two points. A large airlift had to be mounted to supply them, using Junkers Ju 52s and instructor pilots drafted in from the flying training schools. These operations lasted until May, when the aircraft and instructors were returned. But, during the following three months, the hectic pace of air operations in all theatres led to a serious depletion of the Luftwaffe reserve of aviation fuel. Cutbacks were ordered in non-essential flying, and again it was the training schools that suffered.

The diversion of aircraft and instructors, coupled with the fuel shortage, disrupted the training of crews to fly multi-engined aircraft. Front-line bomber and long-range reconnaissance units felt the effects of these changes immediately. For the rest of the war there would be a steady deterioration in the training given to new crews. From this point, each time an experienced crew was lost a unit's combat effectiveness fell by a small but measurable amount.

By the summer of 1942 the Luftwaffe was slipping behind its adversaries in each of the main components of air power – in the quantity and quality of its aircraft and in the quantity and quality of its crews. Yet although the future looked bleak for the Luftwaffe in the medium and the long term, in the short term there were some grounds for optimism. In September 1942 the decisive battle for the city of Stalingrad was still going well for the Germans. The action had drawn in huge Soviet forces and these were being systematically destroyed. From the German High Command there were confident assertions that, with the huge losses it had already suffered, the Red Army was on the brink of collapse.

If a victory could be secured on the Eastern Front, the picture would change completely. Then the Luftwaffe could redeploy large forces to the Western and the Mediterranean theatres to stabilize the situation there. And, having established a breathing space, the Luftwaffe would be able to build up its fighting strength.

The story of what befell the Luftwaffe during the final thirty-one months of the war is told, in photographs, in the second volume in this series.

ACKNOWLEDGEMENTS

It would have been impossible to assemble the material for this book had it not been for the generosity of those who so kindly allowed me the use of their photographs. In particular I should like to thank Hanfried Schliephake, Gerhard Schöpfel, Robert Michulec, Günther Unger, Hajo Hermann, Oskar Romm, Willi Herget, Fritz Stehle, Günther Heise, Kurt Scheffel, Bernard Jope, Hans-Georg Bätcher, Otto Schmidt, Horst Götz, Julius Neumann, Helmut Wenk, Theodor Rehm, Robert Kowalewski, Werner Schrör, Helmut Mahlke, Diether Lukesch, Horst Schultz, Werner Haugk, Wolfgang Dierich and Helmut Bode. To all of these gentlemen, I tender my grateful thanks.

Alfred Price, 1997

POLAND, DENMARK, NORWAY, BELGIUM, HOLLAND, FRANCE

SEPTEMBER 1939 TO JUNE 1940

Junkers Ju 87s of Ist Gruppe of Sturzkampfgeschwader 77 (I./StG 77), together with a Fieseler Storch, under camouflage at their forward base at Oppeln in Silesia, during the final week of August 1939, as Luftwaffe crews awaited the final order to go to war. Scheffel

A pair of Stukas of I./StG 77 taxiing out from Oppeln to attack a target in Poland on the morning of 1 September 1939, the first day of the war. Scheffel

A Henschel Hs 123 ground attack aircraft. Despite its outdated appearance, this type proved effective for strafing ground targets and providing close air support for German troops during the campaign in Poland. via Schliephake

Heinkel He 46 short-range reconnaissance and army co-operation planes, pictured before the war. Thanks to the air superiority achieved by the Luftwaffe over Poland, this low performance aircraft was able to operate effectively throughout the campaign.

Messerschmitt Bf 109Cs of Jagdgruppe 102 (JGr 102), summer 1939.

A pilot boards a Bf 109E bearing the 'Scalded Cat' insignia of Jagdgeschwader 20 for a scramble take-off, summer 1939. A mechanic had started the engine before the pilot reached the cockpit.

Bf 109E of JG 27, early in the war. The oversized wing markings served as an additional aid to recognition, following a series of unfortunate incidents when aircraft were engaged in error by 'friendly' forces. Both sides lost aircraft to this cause. via Schliephake

Ground crewmen reloading the wing and engine-mounted 7.9 mm machine-guns of a Bf 109C of IIIrd Gruppe of Jagdgeschwader 51 (III./JG 51). Scrupulous cleanliness was necessary for this operation, since any grit or dirt adhering to the rounds might cause a stoppage during firing.

Formation pair take-off by Bf 109Cs of JG 51.

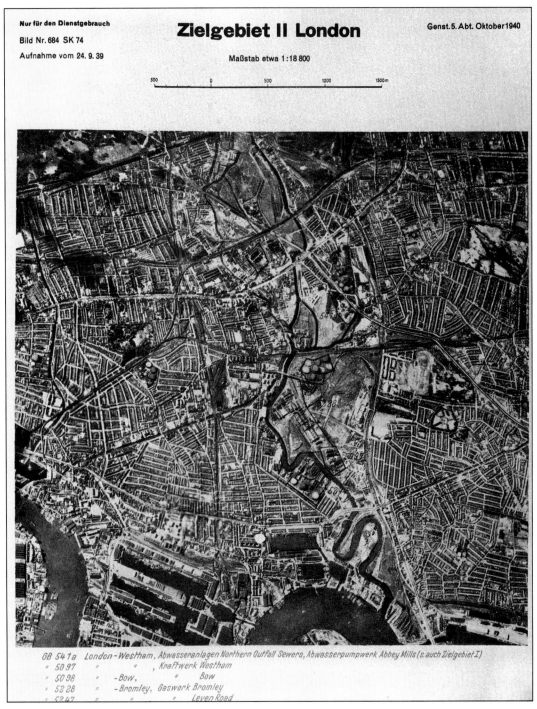

Nur für den Dienstgebrauch

Bild Nr. 684 SK 74

Aufnahme vom 24. 9. 39

Zielgebiet II London

Maßstab etwa 1 : 18 800

Genst. 5. Abt. Oktober 1940

500   0   500   1000   1500m

GB 54 1a   London-Westham, Abwasseranlagen Northern Outfall Sewers, Abwasserpumpwerk Abbey Mills (s. auch Zielgebiet I)
„ 50.97   „   „   „   , Kraftwerk Westham
„ 50.98   „   -Bow,   „   Bow
„ 52.28   „   -Bromley, Gaswerk Bromley
„ 52.47   „   „   „   Leven Road

Reconnaissance photograph of the Bromley-by-Bow and Poplar areas of London, taken during a mission flown on 24 September 1939. The photographic aircraft was probably a Do 17P. At the bottom of the photograph the River Thames and the West India Docks can be clearly seen.

Dornier Do 17P reconnaissance aircraft of Aufklärungsgruppe 22 (Aufkl.Gr 22). Operating from bases in western Germany, this unit flew numerous sorties to photograph defended areas in France, Holland and Belgium in preparation for the German offensive in May 1940. Its aircraft also operated over Great Britain, taking pre-strike photographs of targets.

The Italian-built Fiat CR 32 was the main fighter type used by the Austrian Air Force, before that service was incorporated into the Luftwaffe in 1938. From then on these aircraft served in the advanced trainer role. via Michulec

The Gotha Go 145 initial trainer served in large numbers at Luftwaffe flying schools.

By the beginning of the war the Heinkel He 70 reconnaissance aircraft had passed out of front-line service, but continued to serve in small numbers as trainers and courier planes.

Loading a practice torpedo into the weapons bay of an He 115 during the type's operational evaluation at the Luftwaffe test centre at Travemünde on the Baltic. This relatively slow aircraft was the main torpedo bomber type in the Luftwaffe during the early war years. Due to the poor reliability of the German air-dropped torpedoes at that time the type achieved little in the role. The He 115 served more effectively in the minelaying and maritime reconnaissance roles. via Michulec

Heinkel He 115 floatplane passes low over German warships on exercise.

Engines running, an He 115 is lowered down to the water before a flight. via Michulec

Dornier Do 18G flying boat being lowered on to its beaching trolley. This maritime reconnaissance type was obsolescent at the beginning of the war, and in 1941 most of those remaining were relegated to the air-sea rescue role. via Michulec

Dornier Do 17s of Kampfgeschwader 3 being prepared for an operation.

Heinkel He 111s of KG 1, probably at their main base at Greifswald during the first winter of the war.

Armourers of KG 3 moving SC 50 (110-pound) bombs into position, before loading them on a Do 17.

He 111s of KG 26 during operations from Lake Tonsvannet near Trondheim, during the campaign in Norway. von Lossberg

Loading an SC 250 (550-pound) bomb on the fuselage rack of a Ju 87.

Junkers Ju 87 dive bombers of Lehrgeschwader 1. Although the unit's title implies that it had a training role, in fact it was a high-grade fighting unit, with experienced crews who were tasked with developing tactics for use with each of the main combat types.

Practice formation flown by Ju 87s of Trägergruppe 186 (Tr.Gr 186), spring 1940. This unit had been formed to operate from the German aircraft carrier *Graf Zeppelin*, which was then being fitted

out at Kiel. This Gruppe flew combat missions alongside other units, and when the carrier programme was cancelled it became a normal front-line unit. Bode

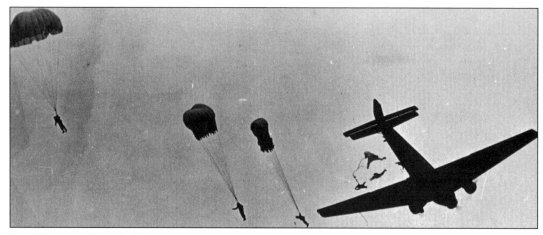

In 1938 the embryonic German paratroop force was incorporated into the Luftwaffe, which controlled all airborne operations from then on. The first use of these units in action was on 9 April 1940, during the invasion of Denmark and Norway. Paratroops are seen here leaving their Junkers Ju 52. The three-engined machine was the main workhorse of the Luftwaffe air transport force throughout the war. Normally it carried up to twelve fully equipped paratroops, or up to 3,300 pounds of cargo. via Michulec

A section of a dozen paratroops parade in front of their Ju 52 transport, before boarding the aircraft for a practice jump. via Michulec

During the campaign in Norway the Luftwaffe also transported army units into airfields captured by the paratroops. Here men from a mountain division don their kit before moving away from their aircraft. via Michulec

German paratroops wave greetings to one of the Stukas that provided them with such effective support during the airborne assault on Holland.

A road convoy under attack in France, viewed from the nose of a Dornier Do 17.

Do 17 of IInd Gruppe of KG 76, fitted with 20 mm cannon in the nose for strafing ground targets. Raab

Ground strafing was a dangerous business for friend and foe alike. On 17 May 1940 this Do 17 of II./KG 76 was strafing a French road convoy when an ammunition truck exploded violently. The German bomber suffered extensive damage, but the pilot, Unteroffizier Otto Stephani, was able to make a normal landing at his base at Vogelsang. The Dornier never flew again. via Rehm

Ripple take-off by a Staffel of Ju 87s. Operational missions often took the Stukas close to the limit of their radius of action. To make the most of the aircraft's limited range it was important to assemble the formation as soon as possible after the leader took off. Where range was critical the aircraft were towed or taxied into position in line abreast at the down-wind end of the airfield, with the leader on the far left. There the engines were warmed up, shut down, and the tanks topped off. At the briefed time the engines were restarted, the leader commenced his take-off run and the other aircraft followed in rapid succession. The aircraft took off parallel headings to keep out of the slipstream and any dust raised by the one ahead. Once the leader was airborne he made a slow turn on to the target heading, flying slowly to allow the rest of the aircraft to move into their assigned places in formation behind him. Once the formation had assembled, the leader increased power and began the climb to attack altitude.

Ju 87s often had to operate from ill-prepared field landing grounds and it was fairly common for an aircraft to dig in a wheel on landing and end up standing on its nose. This aircraft of I./StG 77 assumed the undignified position after landing at Le Mesul-Angat in Normandy. Scheffel

SC 250 bomb (550-pounder) viewed immediately after release from a Ju 87. Having pushed the bomb clear of the airscrew disk, the special crutch mechanism has been pushed back by the airflow and now hangs below the fuselage.

Ju 87s of I./StG 77 camouflaged at their dispersal points at Courcelles, near St Quentin during the campaign in France. Scheffel

Luftwaffe personnel examine a Spitfire of No. 74 Squadron, which had been abandoned intact at Calais Marck airfield. Barbas

Aircrew of KG 76 inspect the wreck of an RAF Hurricane that lay abandoned at their airfield at Beauvais. Remm

Wrecked French military aircraft at the airfield at Escarmain, following its capture by German forces. Unger

Officers of KG 76 outside Notre-Dame Cathedral, Paris on a sightseeing tour following the victorious conclusion of the campaign in France.

A direct hit on one of the ships taking part in the Dunkirk evacuation on 1 June 1940, during an attack by Stukas of I./StG 77. Scheffel

During the campaign in the West the Henschel Hs 126 equipped almost all short-range reconnaissance units.

THE BATTLE OF BRITAIN

JULY TO DECEMBER 1940

Generalfeldmarschall Albert Kesselring, second from left, was commander of Luftflotte 2 during the Battle of Britain. In the First World War he served in the army and rose to become adjutant of a brigade. An extremely capable administrator, he transferred to the Luftwaffe in 1933 and became head of its administrative office. In the years to follow he advanced rapidly and by the summer of 1940 he was in command of Luftflotte 2, the largest of these formations. From his headquarters in Brussels he controlled all units based in Holland, Belgium and France east of the Seine. A German officer of the old school, Kesselring was firm but always courteous with subordinates and greatly respected. To the left of Kesselring is General Jeschonnek, Chief of Staff of the Luftwaffe. On his right are General Speidel, Chief of Staff of Luftflotte 2, and General Bruno Loerzer, commander of Fliegerkorps II. von Lossberg

Generalfeldmarschall Hugo Sperrle, right, commander of Luftflotte 3 during the Battle of Britain. His formation comprised Luftwaffe units based in south-west Germany and France west of the Seine. In the First World War he served in the Imperial Flying Service, and transferred to the army after the conflict. In 1935 he moved to the new Luftwaffe and the following year commanded the Legion Kondor, sent to fight in the Spanish Civil War. In contrast to Kesselring, Sperrle was an aloof figure and a stickler for protocol. Hitler referred to him as 'one of his most brutal-looking generals'. via Dierich

Bf 109 pilots of IIIrd Gruppe, Jagdgeschwader 26. From left to right: Leutnant Lüdewig, Leutnant Heinz Ebeling, Oberleutnant Gerhard Schöpfel, Oberleutnant Josef Haiböck and Leutnant Hans Nauman. Schöpfel

Newly delivered replacement Bf 109 'Emils' for JG 26, France, 1940. They are being painted in the markings and colour scheme used by the unit.

Officers of III./JG 26 discussing the unit's next mission, outside the headquarters caravan at the airfield at Caffiers, near Calais. Seated second from left is the unit commander, Major Adolf Galland. To his immediate left is Gerhard Schöpfel. Schöpfel

The Heinkel He 59, an obsolete torpedo bomber floatplane, operated in the air-sea rescue role during the Battle of Britain. Initially these aircraft were painted in white all over and carried prominent red cross markings to indicate their non-combatant role. The RAF did not recognize

this status, however, and pilots were ordered to attack the floatplanes on sight. Thereafter, the Heinkels were camouflaged and carried machine-guns for self-protection. via Schliephake

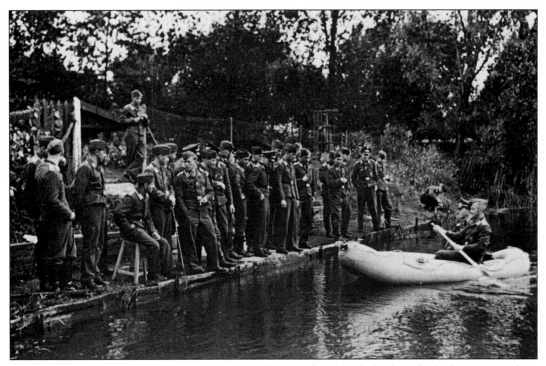

Aircrew of KG 76 trying out one of the rubber dinghies fitted to their aircraft, during preparations for the Battle of Britain. In 1940 the sea-survival equipment issued to Luftwaffe aircrew was far better than that provided by the RAF. Rehm

A camouflaged He 59 floatplane flies low over a rescue launch during an exercise. During the Battle of Britain the two worked in concert to rescue aircrew from both sides.

Intelligence Hoax. Before the war the Luftwaffe had rejected the Heinkel He 100 in favour of developed versions of the Bf 109. The Heinkel fighter was offered for export, however. In the spring of 1940 nine He 100s were employed in a remarkable hoax intended to convince the Allied intelligence services that the He 113, a new high-performance fighter, had entered service. The aircraft were photographed in lines, bearing bogus unit markings and victory bars. The hoax was successful, and during the Battle of Britain RAF pilots reported numerous combats with 'He 113s'. Strangely, although several of these fighters were claimed shot down, no wreck of one was ever found in Britain. via Schliephake

The Messerschmitt Bf 110 was the most effective twin-engined fighter type to see action during the early part of the war. This example belonged to Zerstörergeschwader 1. With a normal radius of action of 340 miles, it promised to be useful as an escort fighter. However, during the Battle of Britain the units suffered heavy losses when they were forced into dogfights with the more manoeuvrable RAF fighters.

Bf 110D fitted with the fixed bulged extra fuel tank under the fuselage. This variant served with Ist Gruppe of Zerstörergeschwader 76 (I./ZG 76) operating from Aalborg in Denmark during the battle. The unprotected extra tank posed a serious fire hazard and following the disastrous action on 15 August, when the unit lost one-third of the Bf 110Ds sent into action, this variant saw little further service. via Schliephake

Smoke rising over Dover harbour, following the destructive dive-bombing attack on the port by Ju 87s on the morning of 29 July.

Bomb damage at Manston. This was the only Fighter Command airfield to be put out of action for any length of time during the Battle of Britain, but it was not one of the all-important Sector stations. The wrecked aircraft in the foreground was a Magister trainer.

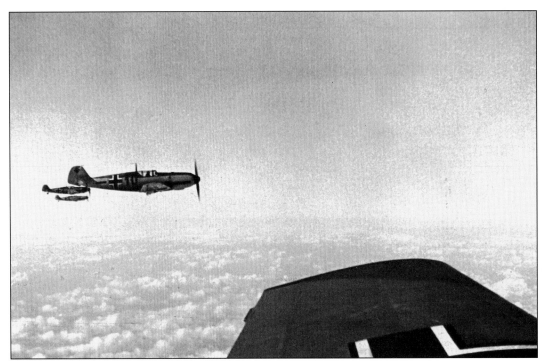

'Schwarm' battle formation of Bf 109Es of II./JG 27, with the aircraft almost in line, abreast and flying well spaced out, early in the Battle of Britain. Neumann

Do 17s of I./KG 76 climbing for an attack on a target in Great Britain.

Ten Hurricanes are seen climbing into position to engage the German formation over Kent on the afternoon of 16 August. They are viewed from a Do 17 of KG 76. The fighters almost certainly belonged to No. 111 Squadron, which delivered a head-on attack on the German formation shortly afterwards. A Hurricane collided with one of the Dorniers and both aircraft crashed near Marden. There were no survivors from either machine. Unger

During the Battle of Britain most Luftwaffe fighter units operated from hastily prepared landing grounds in northern France. Although these had no permanent facilities, in the warm summer weather engineering work could be carried out in the open with little difficulty. A Bf 109E of III./JG 26 has an engine change at Caffiers, near Calais (above). A Bf 110C of I./ZG 76 has an engine change at Laval, near Le Mans (below).

A close-up of the marking carried by the Dorniers of 2. Staffel of KG 76 during the attacks on Great Britain in the summer of 1940. Rehm

Hauptmann Karl Ebbinghausen, commander of II./JG 2, pictured in his personal Bf 109. He was killed in action with British fighters on 16 August.

On 18 August, Kampfgeschwader 76 attempted an ambitious attack against Kenley airfield. First, a dozen Junkers Ju 88s of the IInd Gruppe were to dive-bomb the hangars and installations. Then twenty-seven Do 17s of the Ist and IIIrd Gruppen were to crater the airfield and knock out the ground defences. Finally, nine Do 17s of the 9th Staffel were to deliver a low altitude attack to finish off any important buildings still standing. Banks of thick cloud over France delayed the form-up of the high-flying Ju 88s and Do 17s, however. As a result the 9th Staffel attacked first, and suffered the wrath of the defences. Of the nine bombers, four were shot down, two more crash landed in France and the rest returned with battle damage.

Do 17s of KG 76 taking off from Cormeilles-en-Vexin near Paris for the attack on Kenley.

Aircraft of 9th Staffel seen skirting round Beachy Head at low altitude, before crossing the coast.

9th Staffel Dornier flying below 100 feet over Kent. The town in the background is Seaford.

The northern edge of Kenley airfield, pictured during the attack by the 9th Staffel. Cannon shells fired from one of the bombers are seen exploding around a gun position in the background. The Spitfire in the revetment, from No. 64 Squadron, suffered minor damage.

Do 17 of I./KG 76 shot down by Pilot Officer Alan Eckford of No. 32 Squadron during the high-altitude attack on Kenley airfield, 18 August. The bomber crashed near Oxted in Surrey.

During the Battle of Britain the Luftwaffe mounted an intensive 3½-week campaign against Fighter Command airfields in southern Britain. On each day that the weather allowed, two or more airfields came under attack. Yet, despite the large effort, the attacks failed to prevent effective operations from any Sector station for more than a few hours. Moreover, during this entire campaign, front-line RAF single-engined fighter units lost fewer than twenty aircraft destroyed on the ground. In a rare success, during the combined high- and low-altitude attack on Kenley on 18 August, four Hurricanes of No. 615 Squadron were destroyed (one is seen here) and three damaged on the ground.

Wrecked hangars at Kenley, pictured immediately after the destructive attack on 18 August. Despite this damage the airfield was back in limited use within two hours of the raid. By the following morning the station's two fighter squadrons were once again at full operational capability.

On the afternoon of 18 August four Gruppen with 109 Ju 87 dive bombers attacked Gosport, Ford and Thorney Island airfield and Poling radar station. Five RAF squadrons engaged the force, shooting down sixteen of the Stukas and causing damage to a further six.

I./StG 77, attacking Thorney Island, bore the brunt of the losses. Of the twenty-eight aircraft it sent into action, ten were destroyed and six damaged. This Ju 87 belonging to the unit crashed at West Broyle near Chichester.

This Ju 87 from II./StG 77 made a forced landing at Ham Manor Golf Course, near Angmering. That evening the Home Guard men left the crash site, and by next morning souvenir hunters had stripped the aircraft bare.

Lucky to be alive! Unteroffizier Karl Meier, a radio operator with I./StG 77. During the attack on Thorney Island his aircraft was attacked by British fighters. He suffered eight hits on his body from British machine-gun rounds, but escaped with only flesh wounds. Selhorn

Royal Navy personnel emerging from their shelters at the Fleet Air Arm airfield at Ford in Sussex to fight the fires caused by the dive-bombing attack. Thirteen aircraft were destroyed and twenty-six damaged on the ground, but most were outdated torpedo bombers used for training and were of no relevance to the main battle.

A German reconnaissance photograph showing smoke rising after the attack on Ford.

An anti-aircraft shell bursting below a Heinkel 111 of KG 53 as it headed for North Weald airfield during the late afternoon of 18 August 1940.

Hauptmann Horst Tietzen, the commander of 5./JG 51, with his personal Bf 109E bearing eighteen victory bars on the tail. On the afternoon of 18 August 1940, when his victory score stood at twenty, he was shot down and killed during an action with Hurricanes of No. 501 Squadron. via Ring

A He 111 releases a string of 110-pound high-explosive bombs. These small weapons were suspended in the bomb bay nose-up, and after release they tumbled into the nose-down position.

He 111s of KG 1 during the Battle of Britain.

Smoke rising at Camber, near Lydd in Kent on the afternoon of 11 September 1940. In the background the wrecks of two Heinkel He 111 bombers, one from KG 1 and the other from KG 26, burn themselves out after being shot down during an attack on London.

Dornier Do 17s in battle formation. This formation was designed to be easy to fly, while providing crews with the greatest possible concentration of defensive fire-power in the all-important rear sector.

A He 111 of KG 1 being inspected after it made a crash landing in southern Britain.

During the daylight attacks on London the escorting Bf 109s had to operate at the limit of their radius of action. Several of these fighters were lost when they ran out of fuel, and this one only just made it back to the coast of France. via Willis

He 111 of KG 1 over West India Docks, during the heavy attack on that part of London on the afternoon of 7 September 1940.

The huge fires started among warehouses at the Surrey Docks on 7 September served as a beacon for the follow-up attack that night. The fires were still burning the following morning, and it required 130 fire pumps to bring the conflagration under control.

From the roof of a building in Fleet Street, smoke is seen rising from the many fires resulting from the bombing of the dockland area of London, 7 September 1940.

These images illustrate the weakness of the .303-in machine-guns fitted to British fighters, when used against enemy bombers. On 15 September this Do 17 of KG 76 crash-landed in France with more than 200 hits. That number of hits indicates that at least two British fighters fired most of their ammunition into the bomber from short range. On the original print of the close-up photograph more than fifty bullet strikes are visible. via Rehm

This badly damaged Do 17 from II./KG 3 made it back to Belgium on one engine after the action on 15 September, but was wrecked in the ensuing crash landing. Schultz

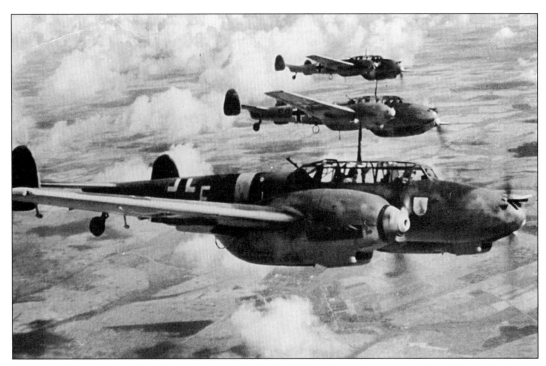

Bf 110s of Schnellkampfgeschwader 210 (SKG 210). This fighter-bomber unit had been formed to introduce the new Messerschmitt Me 210 into service when it became available. However, during the Battle of Britain it operated the earlier type.

Ground crewmen of SKG 210 await the order to load 550-pound bombs on the unit's Bf 110s.

Junkers Ju 88 of KG 54, in its camouflaged pen at St André in France. via Michulec

Bf 109Es of II./JG 53 preparing to take off from the grass airfield at Dinan in western France.

Bf 109Es loaded with 550-pound bombs. During the final phase of the Battle of Britain these aircraft delivered numerous attacks on London and other targets in southern Britain.

Oberst Werner Mölders, commander of JG 51, was the top-scoring German fighter ace in the Battle of Britain. His victory total passed the fifty mark in October 1940, and reached sixty in the following February.

Major Günter Lützow, left, commander of JG 3 during the latter part of the Battle of Britain. On 18 September 1940 his victory score stood at fifteen. To his right is Hauptmann Wilhelm Balthasar, commander of IIIrd Gruppe, whose victory score topped the forty mark when he was wounded in action on 4 September 1940.

Major Helmut Wick, facing camera, had a meteoric rise during the Battle of Britain. In July 1940, as an Oberleutnant, he commanded 3. Staffel of JG 2. In September, as a Hauptmann, he took command of Ist Gruppe. In October, with the rank of Major, he assumed command of the Geschwader. Helmut Wick was killed on 28 November in a dogfight with Spitfires of No. 609 Squadron, when his victory score stood at fifty-six. via Frappe

Major Adolf Galland, commander of JG 26 during the latter part of the Battle of Britain, seated in his personal Bf 109. Note the non-standard telescopic sight mounted in the windscreen. Galland's victory score reached forty on 25 September 1940.

An unusual shot of Spitfires over Snodland, Kent, taken from the Messerschmitt Bf 110 reconnaissance aircraft the Spitfires were climbing to intercept, 21 December 1940. Twenty-three Spitfires from Nos 64 and 611 Squadrons took part in the interception which ended in a long chase out to sea. After suffering severe damage and with a dead gunner, the Messerschmitt escaped and made an emergency landing at Mardyk near Dunkirk. via Fischer

Junkers Ju 86P high-altitude reconnaissance aircraft. This advanced aircraft featured a pressurized cabin and was powered by two highly supercharged diesel engines, enabling it to operate at altitudes above 37,000 feet, where it was immune from fighter interception during the early war years.

Spoils of war. Royal Air Force personnel pumping petrol from a Ju 88 of KG 54 that crash-landed near Tangmere into a private car belonging to one of them. Such misuse of captured enemy material was illegal, but usually those in authority turned a blind eye to it. Lloyd

THE NIGHT BLITZ ON BRITAIN

AUGUST 1940 TO MAY 1941

'Knickebein' transmitting station situated at Mount Pinçon, near Saint Lô in northern France. The station radiated a narrow radio beam at high power, which was accurately aligned on the target to be attacked. The beam signals were picked up by the standard airfield approach receivers carried by all German bombers, and no special equipment was necessary for crews to use this system.

Armourers carry out final adjustments on a 550-pound bomb mounted under the fuselage of a He 111. Note the compressed cardboard 'screamers' fitted to the fins of the bomb, intended to increase the weapon's effect on enemy morale.

A He 111 with a 5,500-pound SC 3500 'Max', the heaviest type of bomb in normal use by the Luftwaffe.

A crew of KG 4 boarding their He 111 for an attack on Great Britain. The aircraft is loaded with two 2,200-pound bombs.

Ground crewmen of KG 1 crank the inertia starter handle to start the starboard engine of a Ju 88 of KG 1, before a night attack on Great Britain.

With four 550-pound bombs carried externally on the underwing racks under the inner wing, a Ju 88 taxies out for a night attack.

A He 111 with two 2,200-pound bombs under the fuselage, taking off for a night mission.

A sombre-looking Winston Churchill inspecting the gutted works of the Silvertown Rubber Company at Winchester Street, 8 September 1940.

Warehouses burning at St Katherine's Dock, following the heavy attack on the night of 11/12 September 1940.

Bomb damage in Leicester Square, in front of the headquarters of the Royal Automobile Association, on the morning of 17 October 1940. The vehicles in the foreground had suffered damage that was beyond even the repair skills of that famous organization.

He 111s of Kampfgruppe 100 (KGr 100), the special night-attack unit which operated from Vannes in Brittany. These aircraft carried receivers for the X-Gerät beam bombing system, employing two additional aerial masts mounted on top of the rear fuselage. The system enjoyed only moderate success during attacks on Great Britain, however.

Feldwebel Horst Götz of KGr 100 in the cockpit of his He 111. Note the 'Viking Ship' emblem of the unit painted on the fuselage. Goëtz

This Heinkel of KGr 100 returned to France after suffering damage during an attack on Great Britain. It made a forced-landing on the beach in Brittany, but before it could be moved the incoming tide and the Atlantic rollers made short work of it. via Trenkle

Armourers loading 2,200-pound parachute mines on the fuselage racks of a He 111. In addition to their intended role of rendering waterways hazardous for shipping, these thin-cased weapons were often fitted with impact fuses for use against land targets.

This He 111-8 from II./KG 27 was running in to deliver a low-altitude night attack on Yeovil when it struck a mist-covered hill near Lulworth Cove, 22 May 1941. The bomber carried a fender attachment mounted in front of the nose and wings to ward off barrage balloon cables. The fender weighed about 550 pounds and required a similar weight of lead in the rear fuselage to serve as a counter-balance. The additional weight and drag of the installation reduced the performance of the aircraft and impaired handling. The device was unpopular with crews, and after a short time it was removed from front-line aircraft.

He 111 of III./KG 26, a night-attack unit that employed the Y-Gerät beam bombing system (note the additional aerial aft of the cockpit). This device proved no more successful than the X-Gerät during attacks on targets in Great Britain, however. The man in front of the aircraft (above) and in the cockpit (below) is Major Viktor von Lossberg, the Gruppe commander. von Lossberg

Propeller change on a Heinkel He 111 of KG 4 at an airfield in France. Note the use of the mobile crane captured from the RAF. via Michulec

THE HOLDING CAMPAIGN IN THE WEST

1941 TO 1942

An early production Bf 109F-1 flown by Major Werner Mölders, commander of JG 51, at St Omer in northern France. The fifty-six victory bars on the rudder indicate that the photographs were probably taken in February 1941. via Schliephake

A Bf 109F flown by the commander of IIIrd Gruppe of JG 2, early in 1941. Note the unit's 'Cock's Head' insignia on the engine cowling.

Bf 109F of one of the Geschwader based in the west, either JG 2 or JG 26. In the background is its camouflaged individual hangar, painted to look like a farm building.

During 1940 and '41 Focke Wulf Fw 200 Kondor aircraft of KG 40 flew far out into the Atlantic, plying between Bordeaux in France and Stavanger in Norway. At that time the Royal Navy was desperately short of escort vessels and the aircraft were able to attack convoys with little risk to themselves. Jope

Armourers loading an 250-kg bomb on the rack under the port outer engine of an Fw 200. Jope

A crew of KG 40 don life-jackets before boarding their Fw 200 for an overseas mission. On the far left is Hauptmann Bernhard Jope, one of the leading exponents of this type of aircraft. *Jope*

Mission tally painted on the rudder of the Fw 200 flown by Leutnant Buchholz of I./KG 40, listing thirteen sorties flown over Britain and ten attacks on ships. via Schliephake

Inside an Fw 200 during an overseas mission. Note the large 66 imp gal fuel tank, one of three such tanks that could be installed in the fuselage for extended range missions. via Selinger

The first unit to become operational with the FW 190 was II./JG 26, based at Moorseele in Belgium, in the summer of 1941. The new German fighter immediately demonstrated a clear edge in combat capability over the Spitfire V, its RAF contemporary, enabling the small force retained in the West to contain the larger RAF attacking forces.

Initially the BMW 801 engine fitted to the Fw 190 was prone to overheat and sometimes catch fire, as happened to this aircraft. Several aircraft were lost to this cause and for a time pilots were forbidden to fly over the sea beyond gliding range from the coast.

The second Gruppe to receive the Fw 190 was III./JG 26, commanded by Major Gerhard Schöpfel, which began re-equipping in September 1941.

In the summer of 1941 the Do 217 entered service in the West, flying with KG 2 and KG 40.

Following the success of the Junkers Ju 87 and Ju 88 in the dive-bombing role, the Luftwaffe stipulated that the Do 217 should also be able to carry out steep diving attacks. The bomber was fitted with a dive brake at the end of the fuselage, but the aircraft was too large and too heavy for this purpose. After several Do 217s had been overstressed pulling out from dives, the idea was dropped. via Schliephake

JG 2, operating in the West, was the second Geschwader to re-equip with the Fw 190. Pilots of IIIrd Gruppe are seen during a scramble take-off, probably at Morlaix in France in the late spring of 1942.

Combat photographs taken by Flt Sgt A. Robinson, a New Zealand Spitfire pilot of No. 485 Squadron, during an action on 4 May 1942 near Ambletuese in northern France. Robinson failed to see the German pilot leaving his aircraft, and he afterwards claimed the enemy fighter 'probably destroyed'.

The three-engined Blohm und Voss Bv 138 flying boat was a highly effective maritime reconnaissance aircraft. via Michulec

Lying at anchor in Tromso Fjord, Norway, the seaplane carrier *Friesenland* catapult-launches a Bv 138 of Kü.Fl 406. The method enabled aircraft to get airborne carrying a greater weight of fuel than was possible with a normal water take-off. via Heise

Bv 138 of 2. Staffel of Küstenfliegergruppe 306 (II./Kü.Fl 306), which conducted operations over the North Sea and the coast of Norway. via Michulec

Junkers Ju 88C night fighters of Nachtjagdgeschwader 2 based at airfields in Holland. During 1940 and '41 this unit carried out intruder operations against RAF Bomber Command bases in eastern Britain. Although they rarely shot down bombers, by forcing the use of minimal lighting at airfields they caused an increased accident rate that took a steady toll of bombers and crews. via Schliephake

During 1942 a couple of Junkers Ju 86R high-altitude bombers carried out nuisance attacks on targets in Britain. A development of the Ju 86P, this variant had a longer span wing and featured nitrous-oxide injection to improve the high-altitude performance of the diesel engines. Cruising at altitudes above 40,000 feet, these aircraft could carry only two 550-pound bombs. In September 1942 one of these aircraft was intercepted over Southampton by a specially modified Spitfire IX. The raider was fortunate to escape from the encounter with only minor damage and, as a consequence of this incident, the attacks ceased.

In July 1942, the pilot of this Fw 190 of III./JG 2 became disorientated during a combat over western Great Britain, and inadvertently landed at Pembrey in South Wales. Thus the RAF acquired an airworthy example of the latest German fighter type. The fighter was repainted in RAF roundels and test flown against each front-line British and US fighter type operating in the theatre.

The Dornier Do 24 served in each of the major sea areas, where it operated mainly in the rescue role. This example belonged to Seenotstaffel 10, based at Tromso in Norway. via Michulec

THE HOME FRONT
1941 TO 1942

The Messerschmitt 210 was designed as a general purpose combat aircraft intended to replace the Ju 87 dive bomber and the Bf 110 in the long-range fighter, fighter-bomber and reconnaissance roles. The Luftwaffe placed an order for 1,000 of these aircraft before the prototype had flown, and the company laid down a large production line. At the same time, production of the earlier types was tailed off in the expectation that large scale deliveries of the Me 210 would commence before the end of 1941. During trials the type demonstrated poor stability, and a tendency to flick into a spin with little warning when flown at low speed at high angles of attack. There were also problems with elevator flutter. After several test crews had been killed, the programme was cancelled early in 1942. Large numbers of incomplete airframes and huge quantities of components had to be scrapped. The Messerschmitt company was forced to meet the costs arising from the fiasco, and had it not been for the company's importance to war production it might have gone bankrupt.

In anticipation of deliveries of the Me 210, production of the Junkers Ju 87 dive bomber tapered off in the autumn of 1941 and in November only two of these aircraft were delivered. Following the cancellation of the Me 210, production of the obsolescent Ju 87 had to be reinstated at the Junkers plant at Berlin-Tempelhof.

The Heinkel He 177 heavy bomber was intended as the standard four-engined heavy bomber for the Luftwaffe. The two engines on each wing were coupled together and drove a single airscrew, giving the aircraft the appearance of a twin-engined machine. via Ethell

The coupled engine arrangement on the He 177 gave constant trouble, however, and several of these bombers were lost following engine fires. A premature attempt to introduce the aircraft into service in 1942 ended in failure, and after several aircraft were destroyed in accidents the type had to be withdrawn for modification. via Schliephake

Adolf Hitler's personal aircraft, a Focke Wulf Fw 200 converted for VIP use and coded 26+00. via Schliephake

Generaloberst Ernst Udet, the highest scoring German fighter ace to survive the First World War, headed the Luftwaffe Technical Office which was responsible for aircraft production. The office was in charge of the development of new aircraft types. Two of the most important of these, the Me 210 and the He 177, had run into seemingly insuperable difficulties. On top of that, in the autumn of 1941, it became clear that industry was not producing aircraft in sufficient numbers to replace losses on the Eastern Front. In October 1941 Udet was reduced to such a state of despair that he shot himself.

At the time the true cause of Udet's demise was a tightly kept secret. The official death notice stated that he was killed 'while testing a new type of weapon'. Udet received a full state funeral attended by Adolf Hitler, far right. One of the leading pallbearers was Oberst Adolf Galland, fifth from the left. The death of Udet led to another disaster for the Luftwaffe. The fighter ace Werner Mölders, on his way to the funeral aboard an He 111 courier plane, was one of those killed when the aircraft crashed near Breslau.

A tranquil evening scene with Arado Ar 196 reconnaissance seaplanes just off the production line at the company's plant at Warnemünde on the Baltic. via Michulec

The Ar 196 was the principal floatplane type carried by German warships of cruiser size and larger. This example belonged to Bordfliegerstaffel 196. via Michulec

Several types of captured seaplane were pressed into service in the Luftwaffe. This Dutch-built Fokker T VIII of Seeaufklärungsgruppe 126 was being towed by a German warship. This was a difficult operation, however, and the aircraft suffered severe damage to the nose and starboard wing after striking the ship. via Michulec

A French Loire 130 flying boat serving with the Luftwaffe. via Michulec

During 1942 the RAF operations to lay mines off German ports began to cause serious losses, particularly among ships transporting high-quality iron ore across the Baltic. Many different aircraft types were fitted with magnetic loop equipment energized by a separate engine in the fuselage to drive a generator to detonate the mines from the air. The loop equipment is seen fitted to a Bv 138 flying boat. via Schliephake

General Josef Kammhuber, the architect of the 'Himmelbett' system of close controlled night fighting developed in 1941.

Leading members of the night fighter force in 1942. In the front rank on the podium, from left to right: Generalmajor Josef Kammhuber, Hauptmann Helmut Lent, Oberleutnant Paul Gildner and Hauptmann Ludwig Bekker. The latter three were among the first pilots to achieve major success in this role.

The Messerschmitt Bf 110F was the mainstay of the Luftwaffe night fighter force during the early war years. These examples belonged to Nachtjagdgeschwader 4 (NJG 4).

Messerschmitt 110 night fighter of NJG 3, fitted with Lichtenstein airborne interception radar. The set had a maximum range of 2½ miles.

Close-up of aerial array for the Lichtenstein radar, fitted to a Ju 88 night fighter. The drag from the nose-mounted aerials reduced the fighter's maximum speed by about 20 m.p.h.

Due to a shortage of Bf 110s in 1942, the Dornier Do 217 was modified as a night fighter and produced in small numbers. Although the type had an excellent endurance, it was sluggish in the climb and it was insufficiently manoeuvrable for this role. The Do 217 was unpopular with night-fighter crews, and after a short period in front-line service it was relegated to the training role.

A 'Himmelbett' night fighter control radar station. The Freya radar in the foreground, with a maximum range of 100 miles, provided area surveillance. The two Giant Würzburg pencil-beam precision radars, in the background, each had a maximum range of 50 miles. One of these sets provided tracking information on the enemy bomber, the other tracked the German night fighter. The tracks of the two planes were plotted by hand on a translucent screen, to enable the ground controller to guide the night fighter into position to intercept the bomber. Scores of these stations were erected, forming a defensive line through which raiders had to pass on their way to and from targets in Germany. As the system became progressively more effective, it took a increasing toll of RAF night bombers. via Heise

The Wassermann radar entered service in 1942 and added to the effectiveness of 'Himmelbett'. This example was situated near Viborg in Denmark. The Wassermann was the best all-round early warning radar to go into service with any nation during the Second World War. The reflector swung from side to side to scan in azimuth, and the radar beam was swept electronically in the vertical plane to measure the altitude of target aircraft.

The Flak arm of the Luftwaffe was responsible for the point defence of potential targets in the German homeland. During 1942, as the RAF night raids on Germany increased in severity, the force underwent a massive expansion. The mainstay of this arm was the 8.8 cm gun which appeared in several versions. via Schliephake

The standard radar equipment for directing searchlights and AA fire was the Würzburg. For its day it was an advanced system, operating on frequencies in the 560 MHz band.

Introduced into service in 1942, the 12.8 cm Flak 40 was the heaviest anti-aircraft weapon employed by the Luftwaffe. This example was the twin installation, mounted on some of the massive Flak towers erected for the defence of major cities.

Close-up of the fuse setter and powered ramming mechanism, to feed the hefty shells into the breech of the 12.8 cm gun.

The Blohm und Voss Bv 141 short-range reconnaissance aircraft was surely one of the oddest looking combat planes ever built. The reason for the lop-sided design was to provide the crew with the best possible all-round view. During flight tests the aircraft exhibited surprisingly good handling characteristics, but conservatism prevailed and the type was never ordered into production. via Schliephake

The Mediterranean Theatre

1941 to 1942

Messerschmitt Bf 110s from III./ZG 26 during the campaign in Greece, spring 1941. Haugk

Do 17 of KG 2 with bright yellow engine cowlings and rudders, which served as identification markings for Luftwaffe bombers during the Balkans campaign.

Italian airmen at the airfield on Rhodes assist with the refuelling of an He 111 of KG 4. Beneath the bomber are two LMB 1,000-kg magnetic mines, probably intended for the approaches to Alexandria harbour or the Suez Canal. via Michulec

Ju 87 dive bombers of StG 77 operating from Prilep in Yugoslavia during the campaign against Greece. Note the yellow cowlings and rudders to assist identification in the theatre. Schmit

Bombs under their fuselages, a pair of Ju 87s of I./StG 77 head for a target on Crete in May 1941.
Scheffel

The airfield at Malemes, Crete, following its capture by German airborne troops. Several of the
aircraft around the landing area had been wrecked or seriously damaged by British artillery fire
before the area was secured. Scheffel

The three-engined Dornier Do 24T flying boat saw extensive use in the Mediterranean area, where it served in the air-sea rescue, maritime reconnaissance and air-transport roles. via Michulec

Bf 109E of JG 26 in the foreground, Bf 110C of III./ZG 26 in the background, at a landing ground in North Africa.

Bf 109Es of JG 27 dispersed around the forward landing ground at Gambut in Libya. The photograph shows the primitive conditions under which the unit had to operate. Schroer

Battle scramble by Bf 109Fs of II./JG 53, the 'Ace of Spades' Geschwader, at an airfield in Sicily.

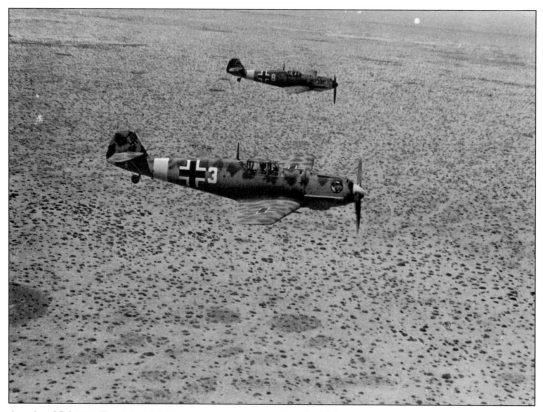

A pair of Bf 109 'Emils' of JG 27 on patrol over the North African desert.

Oberstleutnant Edouard Neumann, the commander of JG 27 from June 1942.

Neumann in the cockpit of his Bf 109G-2. via Michulec

Hauptmann Hans Joachim Marseille of JG 27, the most successful German fighter pilot in Africa. At the time of his death in a flying accident in September 1942 his victory score stood at 158.

Throughout the campaign in North Africa the Germans made large-scale use of transport planes to bring in supplies and fresh troops, and the latter often came under attack from Allied fighters. Here a Bf 110 of ZG 26 is seen escorting a pair of Ju 52 transports over North Africa.

Soldiers deplaning from a Ju 52, after their arrival in North Africa. via Michulec

Ar 196s operating from a seaplane base near Venice. These aircraft, belonging to 4. Staffel of Bordfliegergruppe 196, were engaged in armed reconnaissance and convoy protection operations over the Adriatic. via Rigglesford

Originally designed for Deutsche Luft Hansa to serve on the airline's planned trans-Atlantic service, the giant Blohm und Voss Bv 222 flying boat was built in small numbers for the Luftwaffe. These aircraft served with Lufttransportstaffel 222, and were used mainly to carry supplies to North Africa and evacuate casualties. via Schliephake

Bv 138 flying boat, believed to be from Seeaufklärungsgruppe 125, which operated this type over the Mediterranean during 1942.

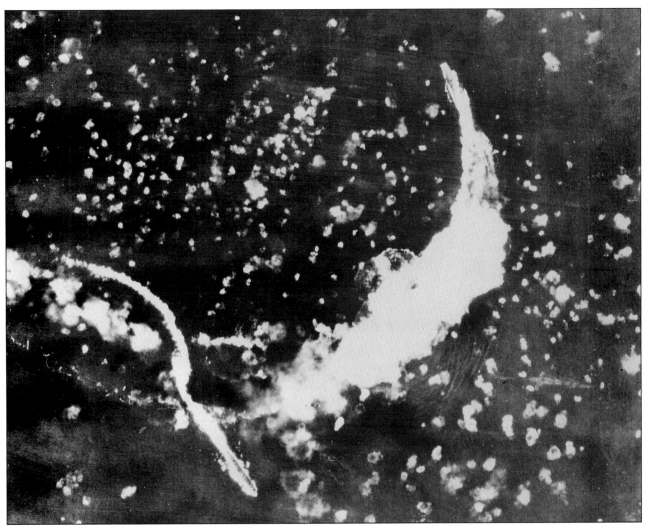

The aircraft carrier HMS *Indomitable* and the cruiser HMS *Phoebe* under attack by Stukas of I./StG 3 off Sicily, 12 August 1942. The carrier, trailing dense smoke after taking two direct hits on her flight deck, is making a tight evasive turn. The damage was so serious that the carrier was unable to operate aircraft and had to return to Gibraltar for repairs.

The Eastern Front

1941 to 1942

Bf 109 'Emils' of JG 52 at Kabaracie, Rumania, in the spring of 1941 shortly before the attack on the Soviet Union. The 'snake' marking on the rear fuselage indicated that these aircraft belonged to the IIIrd Gruppe.

Me 109 'Friedrich' of JG 54 beside a captured Soviet I-16 fighter. The more powerful and cleaner-lined German fighter had a considerable speed advantage over its enemy counterpart, especially at high altitude.

During the early months of the campaign on the Eastern Front, KG 3 flew Do 17s for a short period before the Geschwader re-equipped with Ju 88s. Note the bombs and ammunition boxes laid out on the grass in the foreground in readiness for the next mission (below). Schultz

The SD-2 fragmentation bomb (above) was unleashed at the beginning of the invasion of the USSR. A Ju 88 or a Do 17 could carry up to 360 of these weapons; a Bf 109 or a Ju 87 could carry up to 96. Nicknamed the 'Butterfly Bomb' by the Allies, the weapon was very effective against personnel in the open, soft-skinned vehicles or aircraft on the ground.

The airfield at Schaulen in Lithuania, seen after its capture by German ground forces. Large numbers of Soviet aircraft lay around the airfield, many of them damaged but some still in an airworthy condition. Note the Gloster Gladiator in the background, one of several examples purchased by the Lithuanian Air Force before the war. Lukesch

In time of war aircraft sometimes remain airborne despite having suffered horrific battle damage. This Ju 88 was struck by a Soviet fighter during a combat over the Black Sea on 16 August 1941. The collision tore away the bomber's starboard tailplane and twisted the rear fuselage 40–50° out of alignment. Leutnant Unrau of I./KG 51 managed to hold the aircraft in the air long enough to regain friendly territory in Rumania, where the crew parachuted to safety. via Dierich

Ju 88 of KG 3 at a landing ground on the Eastern Front. Schultz

The Junkers Ju 88D was the mainstay of the long-range reconnaissance units for most of the war. This example belonged to Aufkl.Gr 22, serving on the Southern Front in Russia.

The Focke Wulf Fw 189 tactical reconnaissance and army co-operation aircraft was employed in large numbers on the Eastern Front. It carried a crew of three and the extensive glazing provided them with a good all-round visibility. So long as the Luftwaffe held air superiority the aircraft was highly effective, but its maximum speed of only 217 m.p.h. rendered it vulnerable if it came under attack from enemy fighters.

Bf 110 reconnaissance aircraft of 3. Staffel, Aufkl.Gr 11 at a forward airstrip on the Southern Front in Russia. via Michulec

The Fiesler Fi 156 Storch, with an outstanding short take-off and landing capability, was used in large numbers on the Eastern Front as a light transport and liaison aircraft.

Bf 109 'Friedrich' of JG 53 at a forward airfield in the Leningrad sector on the Eastern Front during the winter of 1941–2.

A snow camouflaged He 111, carrying a 2,200 bomb, on its way to attack a target on the Eastern Front.

Heading east towards the rising sun soon after first light, a Ju 88 cruises over the still waters of the Black Sea.

On the Eastern Front the Luftwaffe frequently mounted supply drops, to take fuel and ammunition to the fast-moving Panzer columns to enable them to maintain the momentum of their thrusts.

Supply containers mounted on the underfuselage racks of a He 111.

He 111s of KG 100 during operations on the Eastern Front.

The Messerschmitt Me 321 heavy lift glider was originally designed for use during the planned invasion of Great Britain. With 200 examples built, their main use in service was to deliver priority cargoes to forward airfields on the Eastern Front. Initially the glider was towed by three Bf 110s flying in formation, but later the specially-developed Heinkel He 111Z was used for this purpose. via Schliephake

The remarkable Heinkel He 111Z (Zwilling = twin) comprised two He 111 bombers joined by a stub wing on which a fifth engine was mounted. Eight of these unusual 'Siamese twins' were built, and used as tugs for Me 321 heavy lift gliders.

On occasions the Focke Wulf Fw 200 maritime reconnaissance aircraft was pressed into use as a transport. However, the fragile, converted airliner was unable to cope with the uneven surfaces it encountered at some of the forward landing grounds.

Leutnant Leykauf of III./JG 54 with his Bf 109F at Siverskaya, June 1942.

Bf 109G-2 of II./JG 54 operating on the northern sector of the Eastern Front in the late spring of 1942. The thaw that followed each Russian winter produced flooding at many of the forward

airfields. This caused severe problems for the flying units. Often aircraft were bogged down in the mud, sometimes suffering damage if they ran into a patch during take-off or landing.

The action around the important naval base at Sevastopol in the Crimea was the focal point of the fighting on the Eastern Front during the spring of 1942.

Major Helmut Bode, commander of III./StG 77, on his way to deliver an attack on a Soviet troop position near the port. Some German dive-bomber units were based at forward landing grounds within 40 km (25 miles) of Sevastopol, and at the height of the action individual crews often flew as many as twelve sorties per day.

Smoke rises from fires started at the port of Sevastopol as a Ju 87 moves into position to commence yet another attack.

The view over the nose of a Ju 87 during its near vertical attack dive on one of the forts at Sevastopol. Bombs dropped from the aircraft in front are seen exploding on the target.

Bf 109G-2 of JG 77 flown by Oberfeldwebel Hans Pichler (right) during operations on the Leningrad Front in Russia, late summer 1942.

Bf 109E fighter-bomber of II./LG 2 taking off from a field landing ground on the Eastern Front.

APPENDIX A
LUFTWAFFE FLYING
UNITS

The Staffel

During the early part of the war the Staffel (plural Staffeln) had a nominal strength of nine aircraft, and it was the smallest combat flying unit in general use in the Luftwaffe. The Staffeln within a Geschwader were designated using Arabic numbers. The 1st, 2nd and 3rd Staffeln belonged to the Ist Gruppe, the 4th, 5th and 6th belonged to the IInd Gruppe and 7th, 8th and 9th Staffeln belonged to the IIIrd Gruppe. If there was a IVth Gruppe (there were a few of these during the early part of the war), it comprised the 10th, 11th and 12th Staffeln.

The Gruppe

The Gruppe (plural Gruppen) was the basic flying unit of the Luftwaffe for operational and administrative purposes. Initially it was established as three Staffeln, each with nine aircraft, and a Staff Flight with three, making thirty aircraft in all. After a prolonged period in action a Gruppe could be considerably smaller than that, however.

The Geschwader

The Geschwader (plural Geschwader) was the largest flying unit in the Luftwaffe to have a fixed nominal strength, initially three Gruppen with a total of ninety aircraft, and a Staff unit of four, making a total of ninety-four aircraft. Originally it had been intended that the Gruppen of each Geschwader would operate from adjacent airfields, but under the stress of war this idea had to be abandoned.

The Fliegerkorps and the Luftflotte

The Fliegerkorps (Air Corps) and the larger Luftflotte (Air Fleet) varied in size, and the number of Gruppen assigned to them depended on the importance of their area of operations.

APPENDIX B
LUFTWAFFE UNIT
ROLE PREFIXES

Luftwaffe Geschwader, Gruppen and Staffeln carried the following prefixes (abbreviated prefixes in brackets) to denote their operational roles:

Aufklärungs- (Aufkl.)	Reconnaissance
Bordflieger- (Bordfl.)	Equipped with floatplanes for operation from warships
Erprobungs- (Erpr.)	Operational Trials Unit
Fernaufklärungs- (FA)	Long-Range Reconnaissance
Jagd- (J)	Fighter
Jagdbomber- (Jabo)	Fighter-Bomber
Kampf- (K)	Bomber
Kampf- z b V (KzbV)	*zur besonderen Verwendung*, literally 'bomber for special purposes', meaning Transport
Küstenflieger- (Kü.Fl)	Unit engaged in coastal operations
Lehr- (L)	Tactical Development Unit
Minensuchs- (MS)	Mine Search (aircraft fitted with equipment to explode magnetic mines from the air)
Nachtjagd- (NJ)	Night Fighter
Nahaufklärungs- (NA)	Short-Range Reconnaissance
Schlacht- (S)	Ground Attack
Schnellkampf- (SK)	High-Speed Bomber
Seeaufklärungs- (Seeaufkl.)	Sea Reconnaissance
Seenot- (SN)	Air-Sea Rescue
Sturzkampf- (St)	Dive bomber
Träger- (T)	Unit formed to operated from aircraft carrier
Wettererkundungs- (Weku)	Weather Reconnaissance
Zerstörer- (Z)	Twin-engined fighter

APPENDIX C
EQUIVALENT WARTIME RANKS

Luftwaffe	RAF	USAAF
Generalfeldmarschal	Marshal of the RAF	(no equivalent)
Generaloberst	Air Chief Marshal	General (4 star)
General der Flieger	Air Marshal	General (3 star)
Generalleutnant	Air Vice-Marshal	General (2 star)
Generalmajor	Air Commodore	General (1 star)
Oberst	Group Captain	Colonel
Oberstleutnant	Wing Commander	Lieutenant Colonel
Major	Squadron Leader	Major
Hauptmann	Flight Lieutenant	Captain
Oberleutnant	Flying Officer	1st Lieutenant
Leutnant	Pilot Officer	2nd Lieutenant
Stabsfeldwebel	Warrant Officer	Warrant Officer
Oberfeldwebel	Flight Sergeant	Master Sergeant
Feldwebel	Sergeant	Technical Sergeant
Unterfeldwebel	(no equivalent)	(no equivalent)
Unteroffizier	Corporal	Staff Sergeant
Hauptgefreiter	(no equivalent)	Sergeant
Obergefreiter	Leading Aircraftman	Corporal
Gefreiter	Aircraftman First Class	Private First Class
Flieger	Aircraftman Second Class	Private Second Class

INDEX